Contents

Any words appearing in the text in bold, **like this**, are explained in the glossary.

KT-225-923

What is drawing?

One of the first things artists learn is how to draw. Drawing is the starting point for most works of art and, in some cases, the final piece as well. In this book we are going to look at some very famous drawings, different ways of drawing, and reasons why some artists prefer to draw rather than paint, sculpt, or take photographs.

This drawing was made by the artist Michelangelo in preparation for his painting on the ceiling of the Sistine Chapel in Rome. This was a huge project that started in 1508. He would have made many hundreds of drawings similar to this one. Michelangelo drew the figures using a **model** in front of him. This is called drawing from life.

Michelangelo drew using a model so he could see exactly what happens to a body when it twists and turns.

Study for the Soul Emerging from the Grave
by Michelangelo Buonarroti, c.1540

"*Ballet Dancer*" Henri Matisse, 1949

Both Matisse and Michelangelo used a method of drawing called **sketching**. This is when artists use small feather-like lines to describe what they are looking at. By using small lines that are at first lightly drawn, artists are able to make their drawings very accurate.

Making drawings more 3-D

To make drawings look **three-dimensional** (3-D) artists use **shading**. Drawings with shading are called **tonal** drawings and can make a flat shape appear more life-like. Here the artist has used a technique called **cross-hatching**. He has drawn small lines in one direction and then drawn others over the top in another direction.

Study for Heads and Arms by Baccio Bandinelli, c. 1545

When there are more layers of cross-hatching, then the tone is darker. When the lines are wider apart then the tones are lighter.

Artists can also create tone using dark and light drawing materials. In this drawing the dark tone is charcoal, which is burnt wood. The light shades are the blank paper and chalk.

Seated Boy with Straw Hat, Study for *Bathers at Asnières* by Georges Seurat, 1883

Light

Artists need to know where to put the dark and light shades as they draw. To do this they decide where the light source is coming from. The light source could be the sun, an electric lamp, or a window. Artists notice where the light shines on an object and they put the lightest tones there. They see where the object is in shadow and put the dark shades there.

Drawing as a discipline

Most artists practise drawing regularly as a **discipline**. This means that artists are always trying to improve their drawing skills or draw things in different ways.

Studies

These drawings of hands were made by the artist Dürer in the 15th century. For each drawing, the artist had to carefully study what he saw in front of him. We call a drawing like this a 'study' because of this.

These drawings would have helped Dürer when he worked on paintings of people.

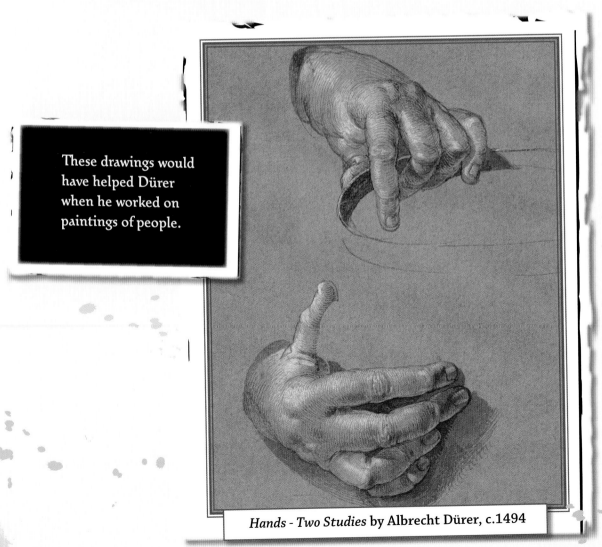

Hands - Two Studies by Albrecht Dürer, c.1494

Did you know?

Artists start a new study when they are unhappy with the last one or because they need to find out what the subject looks like in different positions. Often these studies are practice for a final piece.

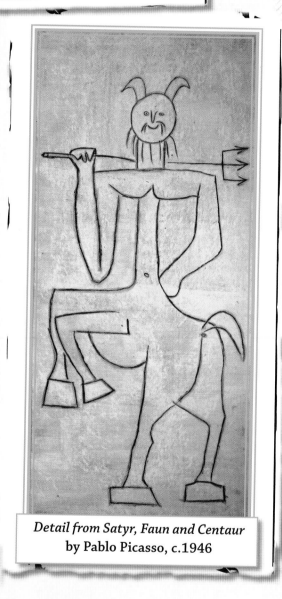

Detail from Satyr, Faun and Centaur
by Pablo Picasso, c.1946

Different views

Picasso used his experiences of drawing from life to imagine what a **mythological creature** might look like. In this drawing he has created a creature called a faun. Picasso liked to think about what a subject looked like from different angles. He then mixed these up in his work.

Art and science

Just as Dürer made studies of hands, artists draw studies of other things in nature. If we look very carefully at how something is put together we can learn how it might work. Leonardo da Vinci is famous for helping us understand the natural world through his detailed drawings. Sometimes he would show the whole subject and then focus on smaller areas in separate drawings. He also sometimes added colour.

Floral Study by Leonardo da Vinci, date unknown

Like Dürer, da Vinci sometimes used his drawings to help him paint.

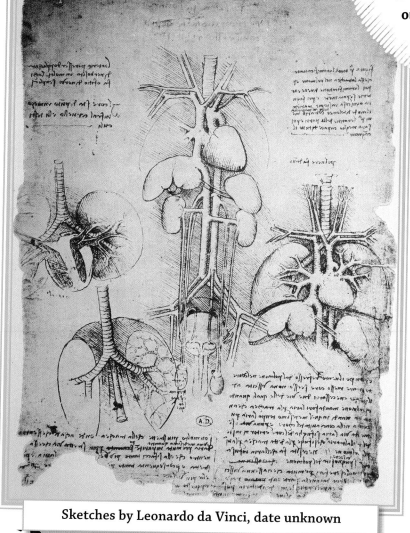

Sketches by Leonardo da Vinci, date unknown

The body

Leonardo da Vinci was allowed to draw various parts of the human
body at hospitals in Italy. This drawing shows a detailed study of
a human heart and lungs. Sometimes da Vinci would write notes next
to his drawings. The notes around the drawing give more information
about what he saw as he studied the subject. He also drew many
animals, such as cows, birds, monkeys, bears, and frogs.

Tricks of the trade

Artists sometimes use a piece of equipment called the camera obscura to help them draw. The camera obscura puts an image of a subject on to a sheet of paper or **canvas** so the artist can trace the outline. It is made of a special box, or room. It is large enough for the paper or canvas needed for the finished artwork to hang inside it. On the opposite wall to the paper is a small hole pointing straight at the subject. Light comes through the hole and makes an upside down image on the paper. The artist traces this image and then turns the paper the right way up.

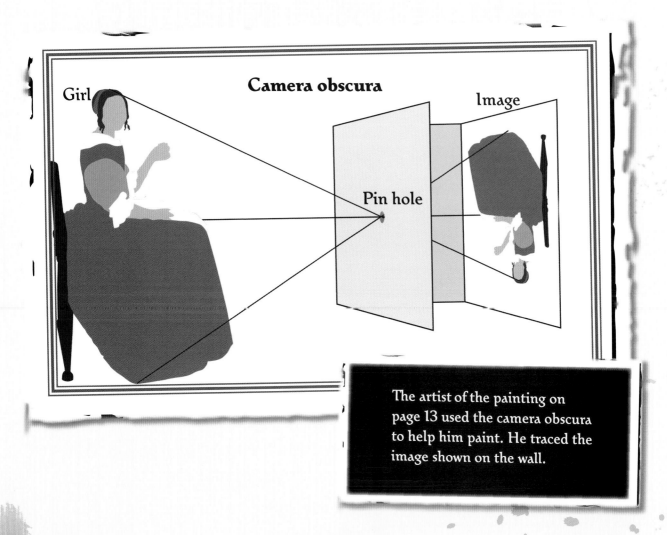

Girl

Camera obscura

Image

Pin hole

The artist of the painting on page 13 used the camera obscura to help him paint. He traced the image shown on the wall.

Do you think the camera obscura is a clever tool that artists use to help them draw? Or do you think it is cheating?

Soldier with Laughing Girl by Jan Vermeer, c. 1659–60

Then and now

The Dutch painter Vermeer made the painting above in the 17th century. Today, the British artist David Hockney has used the camera obscura method.

Research drawings

Many artists use drawings as a way to work out how their final paintings will look. Constable would have made many pencil drawings in his sketchbook before making this full-sized painting sketch of his most famous work *The Hay Wain*.

Study for *The Hay Wain* by John Constable, c. 1821

Because the artist is drawing with paint a practice picture like this one is still called a sketch.

Constable still wanted to
make some changes for the
final painting. Where has
the artist decided to do this?
Can you spot any differences
between the sketch and the
finished painting?

The Hay Wain by John Constable, 1821

The painting shows Flatford Mill in Suffolk, England, where the
artist used to play when he was a young boy. Constable would
spend hours **sketching** different parts of the scene. He would make
individual drawings and small paintings of trees, the cottage, the
people, and horse-drawn carts. The cart in the painting carries hay
and is called a hay wain. He would sketch at different times of the
day to show the way the light changed. With all this information
he was then able to make the final large painting we see here.

What are cartoons?

The cartoons we know are comic strips or movies. But originally cartoons were full-sized drawings that artists put onto paintings or **tapestries**. People who made stained glass windows first used cartoons. They made designs for large church windows and then cut them up into sections to be made in smaller parts.

Leonardo da Vinci drew this cartoon as part of his work on a painting, but it was never used. That is why it is still here today.

Virgin and Child with St Anne and John the Baptist by Leonardo da Vinci, 1499

Before painters used cartoons in this way they drew their designs straight on to a canvas or a wall. Drawing a cartoon on paper first was much better. The artist could change their mind more easily and also their assistants could use the cartoons to draw the designs without the master artist there. This was a big help when artists worked on many projects at the same time.

Most cartoons did not last. When artists put the image of a cartoon onto a wall or canvas they were ruined. The artist made small holes on the drawn lines of the cartoon and then brushed powdered charcoal through these holes with a special brush. When the cartoon was removed the artist joined these dots to make a complete image. Then they could start painting.

Cartoons today

Mickey Mouse

The word cartoon has changed over the years to not simply mean a first draft drawing. It now also means a comical drawing. Sometimes it can be a series of drawings that make up a story. Mickey Mouse is probably the most famous cartoon character of all time. He was created in 1928 by Walt Disney.

To make **animation**, an artist needs to make many drawings. These are then filmed one after the other. When they are shown together, it looks like the character is moving. This works just like a flip picture book. Mickey Mouse animated cartoons became popular very quickly. In 1930 he appeared in comic books, too.

Mickey Mouse comic cover

Compare this Mickey Mouse cartoon with the Leonardo da Vinci cartoon on page 16. They are very different, but can you spot any similarities?

In this caricature of US president George Bush, the artist has focused on certain aspects of Bush's face. He has magnified them to make a comical portrait.

Modern-day cartoon of US President George Bush

Caricatures

Caricatures are a type of drawing that focuses on a person's features and makes them seem larger than life. Artists also use caricatures to tell us something about a person's character. Famous people, such as politicians and actors, are often the subject of caricatures. They can be very funny but also sometimes quite cruel.

Famous cartoonists

Ted Seuss, who created the children's 'Cat in the Hat' character, said that he was a doodler at heart. As a student at school and university he would doodle away all day. He eventually realized that he wanted to try and make his job drawing cartoons. Many children have enjoyed learning to read with the funny cat and his friends. The rhymes in the books are linked to the pictures, so it is easy to work out the story from the images as well as from the words.

Dr Seuss's books have been translated into 15 languages.

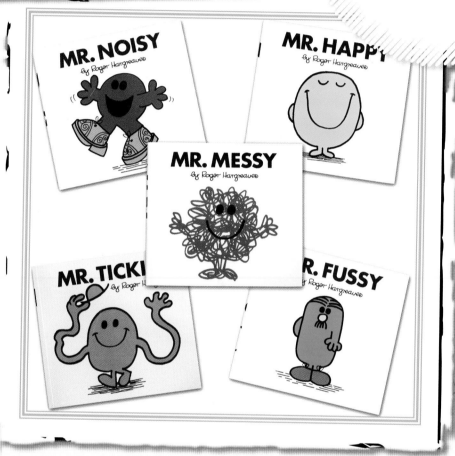

The Mr Men

The Mr Men series began in the early 1970s. In 1981, a Little Miss series was started, with female characters.

The Mr Men characters are all very simple cartoons. Roger Hargreaves drew the Mr Men characters in a way that hints at their name. We call this **symbolism**. Mr Tickle, for example, has very long arms. Mr Strong is a hard-angled square shape and Mr Daydream's body is based on a cloud.

Comic books and TV cartoons

The action hero Superman started as a comic strip and is famous all over the world today. Superman is now also on film and television. This image is from the original comic strip design. Is it any different to the modern Superman image we know today?

What is it about the design of Superman that makes him into a superhero? Is it just his clothes? Perhaps the way he stands or the shape of his body also help us think about his special powers.

Superman was one of the first superheroes to appear in American comic books.

One very famous cartoon series in Japan was created in a comic
book by artist Hasegawa Machiko and has been on Japanese TV
since 1969. All the characters are related to the sea. The name of the
lead character, Sazae, means a type of shellfish in Japanese. She is
a 23 year old housewife who lives with her parents, younger brother,
sister, husband, and baby son. Through the family's daily life, stories
are told about Japanese **culture**. Many thousands of people in
Japan switch on to catch up with Sazae's family.

Drawing on walls

These cartoons have been drawn on a wall using spray paint. We call this graffiti. As long as graffiti is created in a place where people are happy to see it then it can be a very powerful way for people to show how they feel and what is important to them. Some graffiti artists design their own special characters that they use again and again. These act as a type of signature, so people can recognize whose work they are looking at.

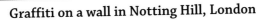
Graffiti on a wall in Notting Hill, London

Graffiti is usually against the law. There are different types of graffiti, though. Do you have it around where you live? Is it like the picture above or do you also see scribbled names and symbols? Or do you have both types? Do you see a difference?

Look at both of these wall pictures. This one was done recently. The other was drawn thousands of years ago. Why do you think each one was made?

Cave paintings may have simply been decoration. Why else might people have drawn on the walls of caves? Could the drawings have had another purpose?

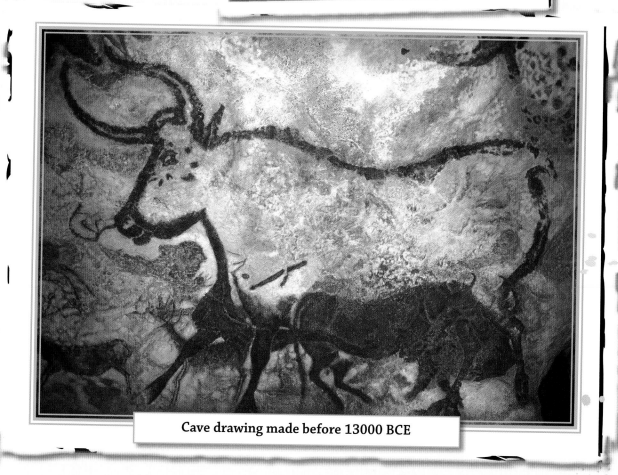

Cave drawing made before 13000 BCE

People have been drawing on walls for thousands of years. These drawings were made on cave walls in **prehistoric** times. The materials the people used were very different to the modern graffiti we can see on the opposite page. Instead of spray paint, people drew the outlines of the animals using natural materials like charcoal and chalk. The images were then filled in with colours made from berries, flowers, and even animals' blood.

Drawing conclusions

In this book we have looked at many reasons why artists practice the art of drawing. We have seen how all artists make drawings at some stage of their work. This can be to work out how a final design may look, to explore a subject in detail, or to use as a final piece in its own right.

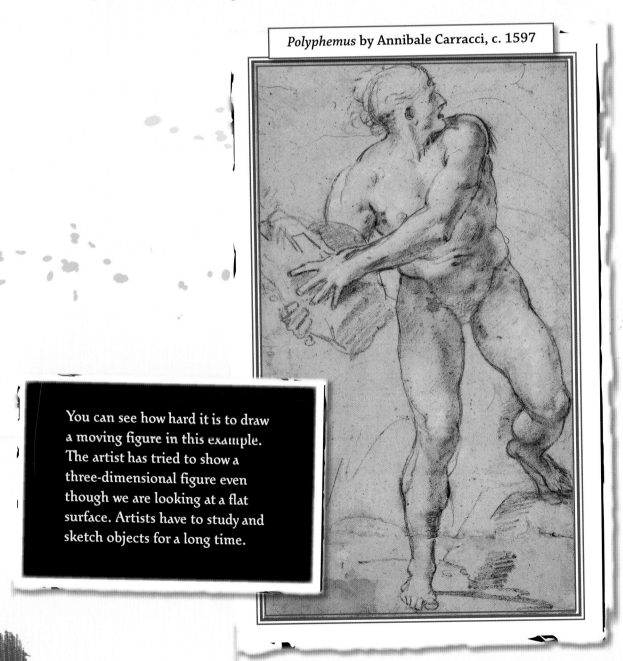

Polyphemus by Annibale Carracci, c. 1597

You can see how hard it is to draw a moving figure in this example. The artist has tried to show a three-dimensional figure even though we are looking at a flat surface. Artists have to study and sketch objects for a long time.

Sketch for *The Races* by Edouard Manet, c. 1865

Most drawings are delicate, and many don't survive over time.
One way for artists to make their drawings last for a long time is
to make an **etching** or **lithograph**. These are drawings made on
metal plates or stone tablets. When the drawing is finished, the artist
treats the plate or tablet with special chemicals. This wears away
the areas where the artist has drawn, and makes a plate. This plate
can be used to print many examples of the drawing.

Timeline

Where to see drawings

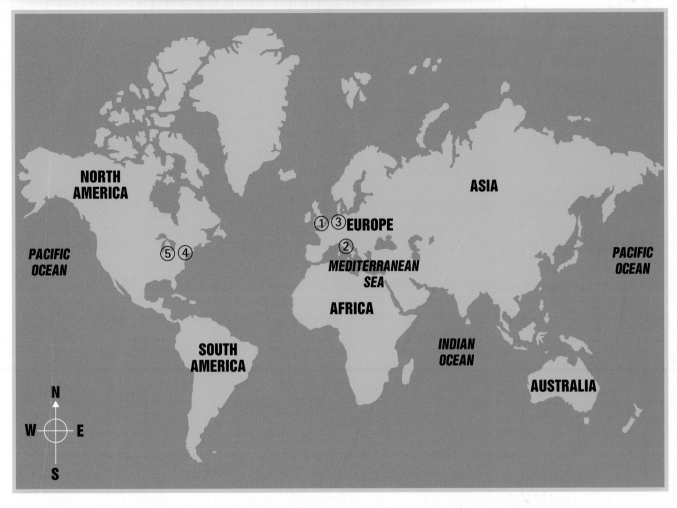

This map shows where some of the artwork in the book can be seen.

(1) **London, UK**
The National Gallery
Virgin and Child with St. Anne and John the Baptist, Leonardo da Vinci
Sketch for *The Hay Wain*, John Constable
Bathers at Asnières, Georges Seurat
See also: The Cartoon Museum

(2) **Rome, Italy**
The Sistine Chapel

(3) **Brunswick, Germany**
Herzog Anton Ulrich Museum: *Soldier with Laughing Girl*, Jan Vermeer

(4) **New York City, USA**
Metropolitan Museum of Art:
Faun and Starry Night, Pablo Picasso

(5) **Chicago, USA**
Art Institute of Chicago:
The Races, Edouard Manet

Glossary

animation   many drawings shown one after the other so they look like a moving picture

canvas   cloth material that many artists use to paint on

cross-hatching   when an artist draws small lines in one direction and then draws other lines over the top in another direction

culture   the customs of a particular time and group of people

discipline   training oneself to become better at something

etching   design scratched on to a metal plate, which is then dipped in acid. The acid eats into the lines on the plate, which can then be used to print lots of copies.

lithograph   type of print made by drawing on a flat stone or metal surface with wax. When ink is added, it sticks to the wax. The stone or metal can then be used to print lots of copies.

model   a person who is the subject of an artwork

mythological creature   a creature from a traditional story involving supernatural or imaginary people

prehistoric   from the earliest times, before records of events were made

shading   adding dark and light to a drawing to make it stand out from the page

sketch   roughly make a drawing or painting

symbolism   something that represents something else

tapestry   material with a woven design, usually hung an a wall

three-dimensional   when something is three-dimensional (3-D) it has length, width, and depth

tonal   to do with light and shade

30

Learn more

Books to read

Cartoons and Animation (Art off the Wall), Richard Spilsbury (Heinemann Library, 2006)

Comic and Graphic Novels (Art off the Wall), Richard Spilsbury (Heinemann Library, 2006)

Line and Tone (How Artists Use), Paul Flux (Heinemann Library, 2008)

Websites to visit

All about Dr Seuss – his life and drawings
www.seussville.com

Biography and works of Leonardo da Vinci
www.mos.org/leonardo

Get inspired at The Art Kids Site!
www.artkids.co.uk

The Tate Gallery kids website
www.tate.org.uk/kids

Index